CW01163725

NATIVE AMERICANS

Helen L. Edmonds

WAYLAND

Titles in the series

Australian Aborigines
Inuit
Native Americans
Rainforest Amerindians

Series editor: Paul Mason
Designer: Kudos Editorial and Design Services

Picture acknowledgements
The map on page 6 was drawn by Peter Bull.
The publishers would also like to thank the following for permission to reproduce their photographs: Bryan and Cherry Alexander 20, 26, 41: Werner Forman Archive 18, 22; David Graham 5, 10, 12, 23, 42, 43; Hulton-Deutsch Collection 8, 34, 35; Impact 11, 14 (Sally Fear), 17 (John Cole), 25, 31 *bottom*, 44 (Sally Fear); Peter Newark's Western Americana 21, 22, 24, 36, 37, 38; Photri 4, 7, 13, 19, 27, 29 *both*, 30, 33, 45; Survival International 15 (Bob Bartel), 28 (uncredited), 39 *bottom* (Bob Bartel); James Wilson 9, 39 *top*, 40; Zefa 31 *top*.

Text is based on *Native Americans* by James Wilson, in the Threatened Cultures series published in 1992.

First published in 1995 by
Wayland (Publishers) Ltd
61 Western Rd, Hove
East Sussex BN3 1JD, England

© Copyright 1995 Wayland (Publishers) Limited

British Library Cataloguing in Publication Data
Edmunds, Helen
  Native Americans.- (People Under
  Threat Series)
  I. Title II. Series
  970.00497

ISBN 0-7502-1421-X

Typeset by Malcolm Walker of Kudos Design
Printed and bound by Lego, Italy

Contents

Introduction 4

The Oglala Sioux 7

Native American groups 12

Traditional beliefs 16

The invasion of North America 20

Threats today 25

Cultural threats 30

Images of Native Americans 34

Native Americans fight back 38

The future 43

Glossary 46

Further information 47

Index 48

1 Introduction

Europeans first heard of America in 1492. This was when Christopher Columbus first arrived on one of the islands off the west coast. But America was already full of people when Columbus arrived – perhaps as many as six million people.

These people were the Native Americans – the first people ever to live in America. They had over six hundred tribes.

MANY DIFFERENT PEOPLES

Native Americans lived in different ways, depending on where in America they had their homes. There were farming communities near the Mississippi river. Some Native Americans lived in small groups in the forests in the north of Canada. Still others hunted on the great Plains in the middle of the country.

◀ *These Native Americans have dressed in traditional costume for a special occasion.*

Since 1492 the Native Americans have faced terrible problems. European diseases killed many. Others were driven from their homes by settlers. By 1890 there were less than 400,000 Native Americans left alive. But then they began to recover, and today there are perhaps three million in the USA and Canada.

This map shows only a few Native American groups. There are many others.

1. Apache
2. Arapaho
3. Cheyenne
4. Chippewa
5. Cree
6. Creek
7. Crow
8. Dene
9. Haida
10. Hopi
11. Innu
12. Navajo
13. Nez Perce
14. Oglala (and other Sioux)
15. Passamaquoddy
16. Paiute
17. Penobscot
18. Pueblo
19. Shawnee
20. Shuswap
21. Shoshone
22. Zuni

2 The Oglala Sioux

The Oglalas are one of the tribes that make up the Great Sioux Nation. The Sioux fiercely defended their lands against the Europeans who came to America. In the end, though, they were defeated. Today, the Sioux live on reservations which the US government forced them on to, after their defeat.

▲ *The Badlands, part of the Oglala reservation.*

◀ *Oglalas packed up and ready to follow the bison herds. The sled-like device behind the horse is called a travois.*

Hunters of the Plains

A hundred and fifty years ago the Oglalas, like most other Sioux, lived by hunting bison. They moved from camp to camp, following the bison. The Oglalas used every part of the bison: meat for food, skins for clothes and tents (called tipis), and bones for tools and weapons.

THE SUN DANCE
Many Plains tribes took part in a religious ceremony called the Sun Dance. This was a way of thanking Wakan Tanka, who the Oglalas believed created the world, for their way of life.

The Oglalas felt close to nature, and thought they were related to the plants and animals they saw all around them.

The Reservation

The Oglalas' old way of life disappeared forever between 1850 and 1890. The US government decided that it wanted to be able to control the Indian lands. It wanted the Sioux to live on an area of land called a reservation.

> **THE BISON SLAUGHTER**
>
> When the US government decided to starve the tribes into submission, the bison were almost wiped out: from 1850 to 1910, their numbers fell from sixty million to a few hundred.

None of the Sioux tribes wanted to live on a reservation. They fought the US Army, and defeated it several times. Then the government almost destroyed the bison herds. The Sioux had no food, and had to surrender.

▲ *Homes on the Oglala reservation today.*

THE BLACK HILLS

The Black Hills are in South Dakota and Wyoming. They are sacred to Native Americans, but were stolen from them by the government, when gold was discovered under them.

Oglala life today

After their surrender, the Oglalas had to move to a reservation at Pine Ridge, in South Dakota. About 2,000 Oglalas still live there today. Pine Ridge is a very poor community. There is not enough land for the tribe to live by hunting, and there are not enough jobs. So most people live partly on money they get from the government.

▼ *These bison live on the Pine Ridge reservation.*

Many of the homes on Pine Ridge are of a very poor standard. Instead of tipis, people now live in small huts. Sometimes the huts do not even have running water.

Keeping traditions alive

The Oglalas have always tried to remember the old ways of doing things, from before Europeans came to America. Children learn about their past in school. All over Pine Ridge, families still breed horses, just as they did 200 years ago. The tribe also has three herds of bison. The meat from the bison is eaten by the Oglalas. If there is any left over, it is sold.

◀ *These Native American children are in a school run by other Native Americans.*

3 Native American groups

No one is sure how the Native Americans arrived in America. Most people think they came from Siberia, by a route that has now disappeared. Then they spread through North America, Central America and out into South America. As they went, the Native Americans adapted to the environments they found: plains, mountains, forests, great rivers and coastal lands.

◀ *An old Native American, wearing a cowboy hat, watches a rodeo.*

▼ *Native Americans lived all over America, even in the frozen areas.*

Native Americans today

Today some parts of North America have no Native Americans living in them. Hundreds of tribes have only a few members left, or have disappeared completely. There are only a few parts of North America in which Native Americans are able to live in a way similar to their ancestors.

▲ *These are homes of the Pueblo tribe, who live in New Mexico.*

The Pueblos

The Pueblos have always lived in the desert regions of the south-west USA. The hot, dry land was unattractive to Europeans, so they did not try hard to drive the Pueblos away.

All through the south-west today, you can still see the homes of the Pueblos. They are flat-roofed houses built using clay bricks. Among the Pueblo tribes are the Hopi and Zuni.

Northern tribes

Another place where traditions have been kept alive is the north of Canada. This is a huge area of forests, rivers and lakes. The summers are short and the winters very cold, so European farmers did not want the land.

▲ *Innu children peek round the corner of their tent.*

The north of Canada is home to hunting peoples, such as the Cree, Innu and Dene. They used to follow the animals they hunted over wide distances. Since the Second World War, the Canadian government has been trying to get them to live in one place.

4 Traditional beliefs

There were many different Native American nations, and each had its own way of life. But there were some things that all Native Americans believed. We can tell what these shared beliefs were from the stories they remember from the old days.

A PUEBLO LEGEND

The Pueblos believe that at the start of the world they lived under a lake. Then a brave warrior was sent to find a way out of the lake. After many adventures he returned, and led them to the place where they live today.

ATTITUDES TO THE LAND

Traditional Native Americans think that the Earth should be looked after. Often they are horrified by the way Europeans and Americans treat the Earth: putting chemicals on it, digging great holes in it and mistreating it in other ways.

The Earth

Native Americans never thought that the Earth could be owned. They thought instead that it belonged to everyone, and that it was their mother because it was the thing that gave them life.

'You ask me to plough the ground!' said Smohalla, a Wanapam holy man, when the government said he must become a farmer. 'Shall I take a knife and tear my mother's bosom?'

Animals, plants and birds

Many traditional Native Americans believe that animals, plants and birds are children of the Earth. They must not simply be used, but should be treated with respect. In some tribes, hunters say a prayer to the animal before killing it: 'Forgive me, brother, but my people must eat'.

▲ *Ploughed fields such as these would have been unpleasant to traditional Native Americans, who thought the Earth should be left undisturbed.*

VISION QUESTS

In many tribes, children who were about to become adults went on a vision quest. They went to some isolated place, were they ate no food and spent their time praying. At the end of this time, they might see a vision that gave them special power or guidance.

Spirits, shamans and witchcraft

For most Native Americans, alongside the world of rocks, trees and buildings there is a spirit world. The Earth herself has a spirit, and so do all the creatures. The spirit world ties everything together.

18

◀ *Henry Crow Dog, a Lakota shaman. The shaman is feared as well as respected. An evil shaman can use his spirit powers to do people harm.*

The spirit world has to be kept in harmony, or there are terrible problems such as hunger, disease and suffering. Most tribes had a special person whose job was to keep the spirits in harmony. This person was a shaman.

19

5 The invasion of North America

Europeans arrived in North America starting in the late 1400s. They came in several different groups. The first Europeans came mainly to trade. They swapped iron tools and weapons for furs. Soon, the balance between the tribes was upset: those with European weapons could easily defeat the tribes which did not have them.

◀ A Cree woman prepares a caribou skin. It was trade in skins and furs that first brought Europeans to Cree territory.

◀ *Paintings such as this one encouraged Europeans to go to America. They thought they would find a good life in the golden west.*

Settlers

The first Europeans brought diseases to which the Native Americans had no resistance. Whole tribes on the east coast were wiped out by these diseases. Their lands were left empty, and during the 1600s large numbers of Europeans began to settle on them.

Many settlers thought that they could have any land where there were no houses. Often such land was part of Native American territory, which led to battles between Indians and settlers.

ALLIES AND ENEMIES

For 300 years after they first came to North America, the British, French and Spanish fought for control. Often they used Native Americans to fight for them, but whichever side won, the Native Americans lost. The fighting was to win land for European settlers, not Native Americans.

21

▲ *Native Americans on horseback hunt bison.*

MOVEMENT WEST

Many tribes only began to hunt bison on the Plains when they were forced to move westwards. So many Europeans were settling in the east that the tribes had to move west to find enough space to live.

Missionaries

As well as settlers, European missionaries soon began to arrive in America. They wanted all people to believe in the Christian religion, and came to persuade the Native Americans to join them.

Most Native Americans respected other people's religions, and at first they welcomed the missionaries. Then they realized that they were expected to abandon their own beliefs. This caused bitter arguments. Some thought the new religion might protect them from the diseases and misfortunes that the Europeans had brought with them. Others refused to give up their beliefs and continued to trust their shaman to protect them.

WOUNDED KNEE MASSACRE

In 1890, one of the worst incidents of the conflict between Europeans and Native Americans happened. The US Cavalry killed more than 300 Sioux men, women and children in a surprise attack. The Sioux were unarmed.

▲ *The memorial to the Sioux killed at Wounded Knee.*

23

The War for the West

In 1848, gold was discovered in California, on America's west coast. Thousands of Europeans began to travel west, over the Plains. They disturbed the bison herds, crossed Native American territory and killed Native Americans on their way. Soon, the Plains tribes were fighting for their lives.

The tribes fought with great skill, even though they were outnumbered. They managed to force the government to sign a peace treaty and leave their territory. So the government decided to starve them into submission by killing all the bison. Once the bison were gone, the tribes had to give in or they would have starved to death.

Red Cloud, one of the great Sioux war chiefs. ▶

6 Threats today

Today, Native American lands take up less than 3 per cent of North America. The Native Americans mainly have poor land that settlers did not want. Now even these places are threatened.

Water wars

Many tribes live in the desert south-west of the USA. They have always had to manage their water carefully to survive. Now, the water is being taken for the growing cities of the south-west. Rivers have been diverted, and underground lakes drained. The tribes are finding it increasingly hard to get enough water to live.

◀ *Native Americans at work on a river bank in the Taos reservation, in New Mexico.*

There are also serious water shortages in parts of the Plains. Without enough water, the tribes fear their lands will turn into deserts where nothing will grow.

In northern Canada, water causes different problems. Dams have been built to create vast hydro-electric schemes. As a result, land that Native Americans use for hunting is being drowned.

▲ *A Cree hunter. The traditional lands of the Cree are now threatened by a hydro-electric scheme.*

26

THE BLACK MESA MINE

The Black Mesa Mine in Arizona has been opposed by Hopi and Navajo for years. As one elder explained, 'Hopi land is held in trust for the Great Spirit . . . if the land is abused, the sacredness of Hopi life will disappear, and all other life too'.

▲ *A Navajo man. Navajo lands are badly affected by mines, including the Black Mesa Mine.*

Mining

Most Native American lands seemed almost worthless when the government forced the tribes to move on to them. Now, oil, coal and other minerals have been found under the ground. Sometimes the tribes have agreed to mining on their lands, often without being told what the effect would be. The mines cause far more damage than expected, as well as pollution and health problems.

27

▲ *Innu people protest at the invasion of their land.*

Logging and oil

Some tribes have been badly affected by logging or oil companies moving on to their land. Large areas of forest have disappeared, or the animals the tribes hunt have been driven away.

Military activity

The US and Canadian governments have both used Native American lands for military activities. In Nevada, Shoshone land was used for nuclear bomb tests. Terrible pollution has ruined the tribes' life.

In Canada, Innu lands are used for military training. Jets fly at high speed just above the ground, terrifying everyone and scaring away the animals the Innu hunt.

THE LUBICON LAKE CREE

In the early 1980s, the Canadian government gave a logging company permission to cut down trees on Cree land around Lubicon Lake. Now, the animals have been driven away, and the Cree have nothing to hunt for food.

'We have been robbed of our land and our freedom. We have seen control of our country . . . taken from us. And now we are treated as invisible, as if we do not exist.'
Rose Gregoire, an Innu.

◀ *Native American leader Russell Means, reading out a list of all the treaties the US government has broken.*

Land rights

Many Native American tribes – for example the Sioux and Shoshone – are still trying to get back land that was taken from them unfairly. Others, such as the Innu in Canada, are trying to get the government to admit that the land the tribes have always lived on belongs to them. Often the government says it will only do this if the tribes agree to sell their land. They would have to live on small reserves, without enough land for hunting.

▲ *Traditional fishing in north-west USA, where hunting and fishing are important activities for Native Americans.*

29

7 Cultural threats

Native Americans are not only threatened by attempts to take their land from them. The conditions in which many of them live, and the beliefs of other North Americans, make it difficult for them to continue to live as Native Americans. Many Canadians and Americans think that Native Americans should live in the same way as other people, not differently.

Racism

In some areas Native Americans are subject to racism. This means they are treated as inferior, and given unfair treatment. Many prefer to stay on their own territory, rather than risk such experiences.

▲ *A shopping mall. Other people accumulate possessions, but many Native Americans own only what they need.*

Education

The US and Canadian government both tried to destroy Native American culture using education. Until the 1960s, children were taken from their parents to attend boarding schools. There, they were made to feel ashamed of their backgrounds.

▲ *A boarding school for Native Americans in 1915.*

NATIVE AMERICAN SCHOOL

Native Americans are now able to set up their own schools. These teach traditional beliefs and history, as well as the usual subjects.

Today, school is a confusing place for native Americans. They learn the same things as other children; for example, to respect the presidents of the USA. But presidents like Andrew Jackson hated Native Americans, and tried to destroy them.

▲ *An Apache girl in the school canteen.*

31

Missionaries

Since the 1870s, the governments of the USA and Canada have given Christian missionaries great power in Native American communities. Missionaries ran some of the boarding schools that punished children for speaking their tribe's language. The missionaries have always tried to destroy Native American traditions such as the Sun Dance.

◀ *Bear Butte, in South Dakota. This is a Sioux holy place, where traditional ceremonies take place.*

▲ *This Native American family in Utah live very simply. They have no electricity and no running water.*

The Welfare culture

Most Native Americans live on lands too small for them to be able to survive by hunting. There are few jobs, so most are forced to try to live off money from the government, called Welfare. The amount of money people get is so small that it is difficult to make ends meet. Many people find their lives very depressing, and end up believing they are worthless.

8 Images of Native Americans

When Columbus arrived in America, he thought he had reached India. He called the people he met Indians. Ever since, people have had mistaken ideas about Native Americans.

The simple savage

To many Europeans, Native Americans seemed to be living in paradise. They were thought of as simple savages, who lived without rules or the need to work.

NATIVE AMERICAN NAMES

Each Native American had a name that had something to do with his or her life: dreams, battles, animals or supernatural beings. For example, a Native American who saw a crazy horse in a dream could be called Crazy Horse.

◀ *A Native American warrior on horseback.*

This cartoon, drawn in 1873, shows a US soldier holding up the scalp of a Native American he has killed. ▶

The bloodthirsty savage

Once Native Americans began to fight to defend their lands from settlers, Europeans began to have another image of them – the bloodthirsty savage. In fact, it was usually Europeans who began killing people as a way of settling arguments.

▲ *A poster advertising a Wild West Show like Buffalo Bill's.*

The Wild West Show and Hollywood Native Americans

About a hundred years ago, Buffalo Bill Cody created a famous Wild West Show. It was like a circus, with brightly coloured cowboys and Native Americans riding round pretending to fight. One of the Native Americans was Sitting Bull, a famous Sioux war chief. Through the show, many people got to think that all Native Americans were like Sitting Bull's Sioux warriors.

The idea that all Native Americans were like Sioux warriors – which had been started by Buffalo Bill's Wild West Show – was continued by the Hollywood film industry. Hollywood also used the old idea of the Bloodthirsty Savage: Native Americans were shown in films attacking settlers, and torturing and killing innocent people.

◀ *A Navajo woman and her daughter. Films often still show Native Americans living in the old way, even though this is no longer possible.*

9 Native Americans fight back

Since about 1500, Native Americans have been trying to defend themselves and their way of life in several different ways.

Warfare

Many Native Americans fought bravely against settlers to defend their lands. Chiefs such as Red Cloud, Crazy Horse (both Oglalas) and Joseph (a Nez Perce) led their peoples against terrible odds, and often managed to hold out for years.

Legal battles

Many tribes have taken their government to court to try and win back land that they say is theirs. Some have been very successful: two tribes from Maine in the USA won back a large chunk of land and $27,500,000.

TECUMSEH

Tecumseh was a great Native American chief who tried to stop settlers taking over Native American land. He led 32 different tribes into battle against the settlers, until he died fighting in 1813.

◀ *Part of the Black Hills. In 1980, the Sioux were offered $105 million in compensation for having lost the hills: they turned it down.*

▼ *A young Innu girl cries, as her mother is arrested at a protest against the Canadian government.*

Other tribes are still fighting in the courts. The Sioux are still trying to get back the Black Hills, over 100 years after the government first stole them.

Campaigns

Many tribes are trying to keep their lifestyle by campaigning. For example, in Canada, the Cree are trying to stop the James Bay dam, which would flood their land. They persuaded the New York Power Authority not to buy James Bay electricity. With no one to buy the electricity, the project may be stopped.

THE INNU'S CAMPAIGN

In the 1980s, Canada decided to build an air base at Goose Bay. The Innu did not want aircraft from the base flying over their land, and began a campaign to stop it that was eventually successful.

▲ *Cree children in school learn the traditional craft of snowshoe-making.*

Education

Since the 1970s, tribes in the USA have been able to run their own schools. Some schools now teach Native American children their own language and culture, as well as more common subjects.

SCHOOLS IN THE CITY

Special schools for Native American children do not exist only on the tribal reservations. In big cities such as Minneapolis, there are thousands of Native Americans. They can also go to schools that teach Native American beliefs.

◀ A young girl dressed in traditional style at a tribal gathering. These are now becoming more and more popular.

Special celebrations

Increasingly, Native Americans celebrate their culture at special events. They wear traditional clothes, and speak their own languages. Many young Native Americans from the cities attend.

10 The future

Return of the disappearing peoples

A hundred years ago, there were only 400,000 Native Americans left. It seemed they would soon disappear altogether. Instead, there are now ten times as many Native Americans as there were a century ago.

▲ *Dancers at the Oglala Pow Wow, a tribal celebration. Pow Wows bring people together to celebrate Indian culture.*

▲ *Part of the Taos reservation in New Mexico.*

There are many problems still facing Native Americans. One of the most important is that they still do not always have any rights over the land they live on. Without land and enough water, it will be hard for tribes to grow.

Many Native Americans think it is important for their cultures to survive, not just for themselves but for the rest of the world too. They believe Europeans and Americans are in danger of destroying the world and everything that lives on it. Pollution from industry, mining, forestry and warfare could all destroy the environment. If other people took notice of Native American beliefs, this could perhaps be stopped.

NATIVE AMERICAN PROPHECIES

An Oglala legend says: '112 years after the last bear leaves the Black Hills will come great changes, the time of Blowing Skies'. If this is a warning of some terrible disaster, we must beware. There have been no bear in the Black Hills since the 1880s.

Glossary

Bison Also sometimes called buffalo, they are large, shaggy-haired animals. There is a picture of a bison on page 10.

Boarding school A school at which the students live, as well as having lessons.

Columbus, Christopher A European explorer, who led an expedition that reached America in 1492.

Culture All the things that make up the way people live, for example: the work they do, their religion, the things they do for entertainment.

Environment The physical landscape: rivers, mountains, trees, grasslands.

Hydro-electric Refers to electricity made with the power of water, for example by damming a river.

Missionaries People who travel to other parts of the world to persuade others to join their religion.

Plains The wide open grasslands at the heart of the North American continent.

Pollution Something from outside that changes an environment. One example of pollution is oil spilling from a ship into the sea.

Shaman An Indian who was given the job of keeping the spirit world in harmony.

Tipi A triangular tent in which many Plains Native Americans lived. It could quickly be packed up, to follow the bison herds that the Plains Native Americans hunted.

Tradition A way of doing things or a belief that people have in common with generations of their ancestors.

Further information

BOOKS

There is a shortage of good books for younger readers about Native Americans. Among the few are:

The First Americans Pamela Odijk (MacMillan, 1989); a good general introduction.

Indians of the Notrh American Plains Virginia Luling (Macdonald Educational, 1978); although old, still a good introduction to the traditional life of the Sioux and other Plains nations, and to be found in larger libraries.

Native North American Stories retold by Robert Hull (Wayland, 1992); a collection of traditional Native American stories.

ORGANIZATIONS

Minority Rights Group
379 Brixton Rd
London SW9 7 DE
The Minority Rights Group produces learning material and information for teachers covering many aspects of minority rights.

Survival International
310 Edgeware Rd
London W2 1DY
Survival International is a worldwide movement to support tribal peoples. It stands for their rights to decide their own future and helps them protect their land and way of life.

There is a group for young people, called Young Survival. For a small membership fee you get a newsletter and the chance to buy games, T-shirts, tapes and other goods.

Index   Numbers in **bold** refer to pictures as well as text.

beliefs, traditional 16-19
bison 8, 9, **10**, 11, 22, 24
Black hills 10, **39**, 45

celebrations 42, 43
chiefs 38
  Red Cloud **24**
  Teasmseh **38**
Columbus, Christopher 4, 34
costume 5, 42

Europeans
  disease 5, 21
  missionaries 22, 23, 32

Hollywood 37

land
  campaigns 40
  land rights 29, 44
  threats 26-28, 45
  winning back land 38

names, traditional 34

racism 30
religion
  shamen 18, **19**
  Sun Dance 8
reservation 7, 9-10

schools
  boarding **31**, 32
  Native American 11, 31, 41

tipis 8
traders 20
travois **8**
tribes
  Cree 15, 20, 26, 28, 40, 41
  Dene 15
  Innu 15, 28, 40
  Navajo 27
  Oglala 7-11
  Pueblo 14, 15, 16

Vision Quest 18

Wounded Knee Massacre 23
welfare 33
Wild West Show 36